Non-Venomous Snakes

Slithering Reptiles

Love of Nature Series

ISSUE 21

Dr. Richard A. NeSmith

Applied **P**rinciples of **E**ducation & *Learning*

APE-Learning

© **2020 Richard A. NeSmith**
Love of Nature Series

dr.nesmith@gmail.com

http://amazon.com/author/richardnesmith

MAY 2025

ISBN: 9798566501444

FLESCH-KINCAID GRADE LEVEL: 8.2

Non-Venomous Snakes

A recent Gallup poll survey found that more than half of the population (51%) is afraid of snakes (*ophidiophobia*). The reason for this fear may include many factors. Two possible explanations include a) everyone can recognize a snake, and b) they have *learned* to fear them. People often fear what they don't know. This book aims to help the reader become more familiar with snakes, judge which ones to avoid and grow in appreciation that snakes are not here to scare or hurt people. They are here to serve a purpose in the ecosystem.

INTRODUCTION TO REPTILES

The word **reptile** comes from the word ***reptar,*** which means to *crawl* or *slither*. The term describes animals that move slowly with their body near the ground. The study of reptiles is known as **herpetology,** which also includes amphibians such as frogs and newts. There are over 6500

different kinds of reptiles. Reptiles have four major characteristics.

All reptiles:

- have a backbone
- produce eggs
- have scales or scutes
- are ectothermic (cold-blooded)

Most reptiles have four legs, except for **snakes** and some **lizards**. The physical features of *non-venomous, native* **(indigenous)** *snakes in North America* will be considered. The information provided in this book does not apply to **invasive** snakes or snakes on other continents.

Range

The overall global status of reptiles is unhealthy, and numbers for many species are in decline. The leading causes of their decline include habitat loss, invasive species, pollution, and climate change.

In North America, no reptiles are found at or above the 60°N latitude. These coordinates are just short of the Arctic Circle. However, two species of garter snakes (Thamnophis) do live as far north as 55°N in western Canada. Numerous species of reptiles only begin appearing just appearing just  south of 40°N latitude. The reason for this *line of demarcation* is that as **_cold-blooded_** animals, they cannot survive long-term exposure to freezing temperatures. The temperature range at those latitudes explains this boundary and why most snakes worldwide live near the tropics. This concept will be further discussed under characteristics.

Characteristics

By definition, a snake is a *limbless*, elongated reptile that is closely related to lizards. All snakes are **carnivorous** animals, and many species produce **venom**, which helps to kill their prey. Being reptiles, they are cold-blooded, lay eggs, and have scales. All snakes are of the suborder **Serpentes** (from *serpent*) and are distinguished from legless lizards by their lack of eyelids and external ears. They breathe air with lungs and have skin made up of specialized dry scales or bony plates/**scutes** (or both). And, they lay *leathery eggs* on dry land.

There are approximately *3,500 species* of snakes **worldwide,** of which only about 600 are venomous. About

50 species of snakes are found in the United States. Alaska and Hawaii are the only states that do not have snakes.

Snakes are easily divided into two groups: **venomous** and **non-venomous**. Of that number, 21 snake species in the US are *venomous*, meaning they produce a **neurotoxin** that affects the bitten victim's nervous system. So, *less than* half of the snakes in the US are dangerous to humans. Here, we will consider the **non-venomous** snakes.[1] Nevertheless, in order to do so, we must be able to identify what snakes are venomous and which are not.

Two-headed snakes do not survive long in the wild . These were adopted and now in captivity.

Biologists and zoologists identify organisms using a **dichotomous key**. This tool seeks simple identification by limiting choices down to *two simple factors*: the name **dichotomous key** (for the stem di- means two). For example, a simple dichotomous choice might be whether the animal's pupils are round or slit? Once that has been determined, the key then sends the observer to other similar options.

---

[1] Note that the term used is "venomous" and not "poisonous." If you eat something that is toxic, then it is poisonous. If something bites you that is toxic, that is venomous.

The simpler the choices, the easier to identify. As you can imagine, not all choices are simple, and not all dichotomous keys have just two options. But, when choosing between alternatives, it guides the observer onto the next characteristic to consider. Below is an *example* of a dichotomous key used by some for keying out lizards. It will provide us with some understanding of how important and useful a systematic observation of characteristics is to properly identify an organism.

In our example key, one could take a specimen looking like a lizard and simply go to the first step, **1a**, and see if the animal had smooth, flat, and shiny scales. If the answer is "yes," then the key directs one to move on to the second characteristic, #2. If the answer is *no*, then progress to **1b**. Observing the animal now brings us to determine if this animal has rough, keeled, and pointed scales.[2] This would be a *determining factor* because the key has identified, based on the characteristics, that this specimen is a Northern Fence Lizard. The genus-species is Sceloporus *undulates.*

Key to the species of Lizards[3]	
1.a Scales smooth, flat, and shiny	Go to 2
1.b Scales are rough, keeled, and pointed	Northern Fence Lizard Sceloporus *undulatus*
2.a. Broad dark brown stripe on each side of the body bordered by thin light stripes above and below it, making four light stripes in total, one postmental scale, young have blue tails	Coal Skink Eumeces *anthracinus*
2.b. Often five light stripes which are wider than in the coal skink, adult males, may have stripes that are faded and a reddish head, two postmental scales, and young have blue tails	Five-Lined Skink Eumeces *fasciatus*

This method is called *keying out* the organism, and there are similar keys for every class of animal on the planet. Sometimes the choices are easy to make. Others require training and dissecting microscopes to be able to see various body parts on the animal. Some keys are short (like the example using the Northern Fence Lizard, whereas some can go on and on. To correctly and accurately identify snakes down to the genus species often requires *keying* the snakes

---

[2] Keeled means there is an elevated ridge down the center of the scale or scute.
[3] This is simply an EXAMPLE of a biology key and these are often prepared for citing a particular state or region. As an example, do NOT attempt to use this for the actual keying of any snake or lizard.

out.[4] Keys work from being very general to becoming more specific. Sometimes the only difference from one species to another is a single final characteristic.

The most significant problem with identifying snakes with generalized characteristics is *they do not always follow the rule for all types of snakes!* It is sort of like buying a used car: Buyer beware! Do not carelessly handle just any snake you find in the wild because you have identified it to be a plain and harmless water snake, when in fact, you discover the hard way that it just might be a juvenile water moccasin. The rule of thumb with snakes is to *err on the side of caution.*

Each year over 7,000 Americans are bitten by venomous snakes. Fortunately, the chances of dying from being bitten

---

[4] For those who just find the *keying out* of snakes very fascinating, there are many sites online to assist with this. One can be found at: https://www.floridamuseum.ufl.edu/herpetology/fl-snakes/identification

by a venomous snake are almost none (one in 50 million).[5] The University of Florida Wildlife Johnson Lab assures us

---

[5] The chances of dying from a venomous snakebite in the United States is nearly zero, because we have available, high-quality medical care in the U.S. Fewer than one in 37,500 people are bitten by venomous snakes in the U.S. each year (7-8,000 bites per year), and only one in 50 million people will die from snakebite (5-6 fatalities per year). Provided by: https://bit.ly/3nmR9ra

that "you are nine times more likely to die from being struck by lightning than to die of venomous snakebite."

However, some essential and general characteristics can be used to identify many snakes. Here are a few of those.

1.   **long, slender bodies**

2.   **rounded heads**

3.   **round pupils**[6]

4.   **usually swim with body submerged**

The problem with *rules of thumb* is that snakes do not read, so they may not follow your rules. However, knowing your geographical area and the types of snakes found there

dramatically reduces the amount of guessing done. With practice, one can become capable of the primary

---

[6] Note: The coral snake is the only round-pupil venomous snake.

identification and differences between venomous and non-venomous snakes.

Knowing that snakes are reptiles, then we know that snakes are cold-blooded (**poikilotherm**). So they cannot function or metabolize at temperatures below 65° Fahrenheit (18° Celsius). As the weather cools in autumn and turns cold in winter, snakes become less active and more lethargic. During the winter months, snakes and other reptiles will enter **brumation**. While this is similar to **hibernation**, brumation is different.

During brumation, a snake's **metabolism** and heart rate slow down as its body temperature lowers with the winter climate. The temperature change brings about biological and physiological (*chemical*) changes in the snake's body. These changes mean that the energy needed from food to survive decreases. Less food is required, but this comes with a severe trade-off; **lethargy**.

Brumation is an incomplete form of *hibernation* where animals do not sleep for long periods. Instead, they are awake but very lethargic or sluggish. This experience might be similar to when one is at school or work and yet feels like they almost cannot keep their eyes open. It can seem like a mental fog causing a slow reaction to the environment. Only, for animals and snakes, their entire **metabolism** has

slowed down so that their bodies are unenergetic and inactive, requiring less energy for survival. Such a state of being is a vulnerable period, and so most of them seek out dens or other places to hide and lay low. For the most part, they seek a warmer and safer place where they will not be disturbed or become prey to another.

When snakes brumate in the wild, they typically go into warm places such as dens made by squirrels, rodents, gopher tortoises, foxes, armadillos, bears, or places where other snakes have bedded down. They will also burrow in tree stumps, caves, and deep caverns. They seek shelters or dens in tree hollows, under logs, leaf litter, underground holes, rock outcroppings, and cavities that other animals have abandoned. It is not entirely uncommon during the winter to find that snakes will even share dens with other animals and utilize their body heat to survive. Talk about *strange bed-fellows*! Such dens or shelters can consist of an entire family of some animal along with their offspring. The snake has no preference for what kind of company it shares with, just that it has the body heat to survive.

Dens are not easily found in urban and suburban areas. So snakes will brumate in crawl spaces, garages, basements, boiler rooms, attics, woodpiles, open pipes or culverts, barns, sheds, storage spaces, or even on car engines to keep warm. However, stumbling upon one of these dormant snakes can produce quite a fright as they are silent and difficult to spot. These snakes are often present but missed by homeowners. Even in the brumation stage, if disturbed, they will feel threatened and can bite. Just exercise caution if you are moving boxes or storage items that have not been used or moved for some time.

We have warned that *rules of thumb* are just references to assist in identifying venomous and non-venomous snakes. Now we will see why this is true.

- **long, slender bodies**

Most non-venomous snakes are long and slender, whereas the venomous ones appear thicker and look fatter. The *exception* is that some nonvenomous snakes, such as water snakes, can bulk up and seem just as thick in diameter.

The venomous coral snake has round pupils just like nonvenomous snakes.

- **rounded heads**

Most non-venomous snakes have rounded heads instead, unlike the venomous pit vipers. The venomous viper snake's head tends to be triangular-shaped due to the heat-sensory pits between the nostril and the eye and the venom's storage organs.[7] The problem here is that some nonvenomous snakes, like water snakes and hognose

---

[7] Most wide snake heads are so because they contain the venom glands. Some venomous snakes, however, do not have triangular-shaped heads because their venom is stored elsewhere.

snakes, will mimic the viper's triangular head when threatened or under attack. A nonvenomous snake at rest will have a rounded head, but you may see their head become more triangular-shaped when you approach.

- **round pupils**

The most used rule of thumb for snakes is the rounded shape of their pupil. This one faces two shortcomings. First, there is the exception of the **coral snake**, which is venomous and yet possesses roundish eyes. Secondly, a snake's pupil shape depends on the time of day they are active. **Diurnal** snakes (those active during the day) tend to have round pupils. **Nocturnal** (those active during the night)

have more often slits or "cat-eyes" with an oblong shape with peaked ends in the center of their eye.

- **usually swim with body submerged**

All snakes can swim, but not all snakes live in or encounter water. Most snakes found in water in North America are *not* venomous. The cottonmouth moccasin is the only venomous snake in the United States that spends a lot of time in the water. When they swim, most of their body is floating along the waterline. Non-venomous snakes, on the contrary, do not tend to swim-float on *top* of the water as such. This is partly due to the size and shape of the non-venomous snakes and their low body mass index (BMI). Less fat—less buoyancy.

Instead, when a nonvenomous water snake swims, the head will be above the surface, but the body will not be visible as it is down in the water. Water snakes are not harmful to humans. They can have dark bands and are often mistaken for copperheads or cottonmouth, but these snakes are not venomous. When agitated, however, they may flatten their head and bite.

Habitats

Apart from not existing above that "cold" line, snakes live in just about *any* environment. They are particularly numerous in forests, especially tropical forest and grassland ecosystems. However, snakes and other reptiles are the most successful vertebrates in some of the harshest and inhospitable environments, including **deserts**. They also thrive in freshwater and marine ecosystems. Some snakes live in the sea all of their lives or share their time between land and sea. Snakes can dive and swim underwater. Some nonvenomous snakes live entirely, or almost wholly, underground their entire lives.

Snakes often nest in tall grasses, in piles of rocks, under

debris, and in areas where there is frequent rodent activity. Likewise, sheltering in tree hollows, under logs, leaf litter, underground holes, rock outcroppings, and cavities that have been abandoned by other animals is quite common. Water snakes live near any water source, including rivers, lakes, ponds, and marshes. They prefer relatively slow or quiet waters. They like to bask in the sun to regulate body temperature, so they tend to locate in areas that are not excessively shaded.

Diet

All snakes are **carnivores** and all stalk and hunt for their prey. However, they will eat **carrion**. Each has its own issues. Trying to eat some animals can be dangerous to the snake, but eating some dead or decaying animals could cause illness or death. Pet snakes are often fed dead animals and have no hesitancy in consuming them if hungry. As with

many animals, snakes are ***opportunistic*** feeders. Should a snake come across a dead frog, it will not reject it just because it is dead.

Obtaining food often involves hunting, stalking, and securing their prey. For example, upon catching a mouse, the snake will wrap its body around the victim. This technique is described as ***coils*** or wrapping its coils around the prey. It wraps its long, elongated body around the mouse as if creating circular rings. The non-venomous snake, having

secured the mouse, tightens (*constricts*) the rings. Longitudinal and circular muscles apply pressure slowly on the mouse's body, reducing oxygen intake and eventually crushing its lungs. As the mouse fights for its life, it tries to breathe more rapidly. Upon each exhalation (expiration), the snake tightens the coil a little more around the mouse's body.

This **constriction** continues for several minutes.[8] Eventually, the mouse is no longer able to breathe and *loses* **consciousness**. The snake will continue to hold tight until the mouse finally goes into shock or dies from suffocation. Not all prey is dead when swallowed.

Once the mouse becomes stunned, the snake will release its grip and rest for a period. Then it will begin to position itself to swallow the mouse whole, headfirst. Before swallowing, the snake will instinctively use its nostrils and tongue to locate the animal's smell of saliva. Snakes have tiny teeth, but

---

[8] Snakes that kill prey in this manner are called *constrictors*.

they cannot chew their food. Some prey is quite large, but the difficulty is not always in overall size but the width of the prey's shoulder and limbs. Once the snake has located the animal's head, it begins to open its jaws and begin taking the head into its mouth.

Unlike most animals, snakes do not have a chin. They have a jawbone (**maxilla**). Whereas a human's jawbone has a simple joint that pivots in one place, a snake's jaw has two pivot points. These pivotal joints (connections) are located at either end of the **quadrate bone**. This bone is *detached* and is held loosely in place by **ligaments**. The jawbone lies beneath the surface of the face, covered by skin and muscle. It also acts as a *receiver* of surface vibrations (rather than sound) by bone conduction.

The flexibility of this skull and jaw permits the snake to swallow large and bulky prey. However, the misconception that snakes "unhinge" their jaw is not valid. The snake does

not unhinge or dislocate its jaw. But these **ligaments** (which are very elastic in nature) allow the two halves of the lower jaw the ability to move independently. So, the ligaments determine how wide the mouth can open. Depending on the size of the prey, swallowing food whole can take minutes or hours. A snake may digest a small mouse at a suitable warm temperature in two or three days, or a deer may require weeks to digest.

The largest animal swallowed by a snake on record was a young whitetail deer weighing 35 lbs. (16 kg) swallowed by a 32 lbs. (14 kg) Burmese python in Florida.[9] Snakes may occasionally start eating something and then abandon it after realizing it is just too large.[10]

After ingesting large meals, a snake will seek to hide and remain low-key and inactive for some time, not requiring another meal for days or weeks. Everything consumed is digested, including bones, flesh, organs, and body fluids.

---

[9] According to the Conservancy of Southwest Florida.
[10] One of the dangers of eating an animal too large is that if the animal begins to rot/decay before it is digested, the snake would become ill and itself die for the toxins produced during decay.

Scales, teeth, and anything made of **keratin** or **enamel** will be passed in the feces.

Sometimes when striking at something solid, the under jaw gets caught on the upper teeth. This problem causes discomfort and temporarily disables the snake until readjusted.

Snakes eat eggs, insects, birds, amphibians, reptiles (including other snakes), and small fish. They will also eat small mammals, such as squirrels, rats, and mice. Rat snakes, as their name indicates, often prey on rats. There are many species of rat snakes. The black rat snake[11], the longest snake in North America, can grow to be over eight feet long. This black snake is found in the central and western United States. The corn snake[12] is a patterned orange snake that lives in the southeastern US. It does not eat corn but owes its name to its habit of living near stored grain where lots of rats and vermin live. Farmers have used corn snakes to control rodent populations since at least the late 17th century.

Snakes do have the capacity to drink water but do not do so regularly. And, some snakes in the desert may live their entire life without ever having

---

[11] Pantherophis *obsoletus*
[12] Pantherophis *guttatus*

taken a drink.[13] Most fluids are obtained from the food consumed.

Behavior

Being cold-blooded, the first behavior, and most  predominant for the non-venomous snakes, is regulating their body temperature. If the snake becomes too cold, then enzymes involved in metabolism fail to function properly.[14] This causes sluggishness in the animal's entire body. Too hot or overheating, and they begin denaturing those enzymes and **proteins** needed for health and life itself. They, like all reptiles, will move in and out of the sunshine multiple times a day. Water snakes will use the water and shade to cool their body temperatures, whereas land snakes will use the shade or an underground cave or burrow. Those living underground will have a more steady temperature range[15] but may shift their location accordingly.

Snakes rely significantly on their **senses** to track and catch their prey, as well as for defense and survival.

---

[13] Some desert snakes have been found to collect and drink the dew, snow, or rare rainfall from off of their own bodies.

[14] Enzymes function normally within a given range. Too much heat or not enough heat can cause them to not function in the metabolic process as needed.

[15] Soil temperatures underground are more constant, consistent and slower to change than above ground.

- **Sight**

Snakes are not blind, but their eyesight is so poor they may

as well be. They see shapes and *motion*, not details. Many amphibians and reptiles that spend long periods underground typically have reduced vision. Snakes have unblinking, lidless eyes without eyelids that are each protected by a *transparent scale* called a **spectacle** or **eye cap**. Upon seeing a skin shed by a snake, one can easily see this scaled covering that protects the eye.

- **Hearing**

Snakes are deaf and lack ear openings (**orifices**).[16] They cannot hear air frequency-induced sounds. However, they do *feel* very low-frequency *vibrations* via the bone conduction in the lower jaw. So, a snake may not see you coming, and it might not hear you approaching, either. It may feel you nearby if the ground vibration results.

Vibrations may be felt from the ground, quickly signaling an approaching animal. The snake's tongue begins flickering rapidly to assess whether to attack, remain hidden, *stand its*

---

[16] Displays of Indian snake charmers playing are all for effect for the cobras do not hear the sound and unless a very low frequency, cannot feel it either.

ground, or flee. Snakes, with a few rare exceptions, do not chase humans. Most snakes, however, will stand their ground. Determining a *friend* or *foe* is the difference between life and death.

- **Smell**

The snake's imperfect and minimal vision, with limited deafness, often causes a heavy reliance on **touch** and **smell** for most of its activities. Snakes do have noses and nostrils,

and they breathe through them just as most animals do. But they use their forked tongues for *collecting* chemicals from the air or ground.

The sense of taste and smell are closely related. However, for snakes, *the tongue does not have receptors for taste or smell.* Instead, these receptors are in the **vomeronasal** (VNO), also called Jacobson's Organ, which is in the roof of the mouth. Here the **olfactory** (smell) sense organ is located in the soft tissue of the **nasal septum**.

The tongue will gather up the odors in the air and bring them to the roof of the mouth, where the VNO then sends the signal to the brain. The VNO enables

a snake to hunt and track prey and identify enemies that might be its predator. When the snake's tongue is inserted into the Jacobson's organ ducts, each fork's scents are analyzed *independently*. This feature guides the snake in knowing which direction to travel based on which of the two forks deposited a higher concentration of the scent.

During mating season, male snakes also use the VNO to detect the **pheromones** of female snakes. Snakes can also follow their own pheromone trail to identify their way back to their den.

- **Movement**

Despite having no limbs, snakes are very mobile and agile. They can move in a range of different ways for different purposes and use various movements simultaneously. Snakes move in one of five ways, depending on the surface area they are occupying.

❶ *lateral undulation:* wave-like movement patterns which propel it forward;

② *sidewinding:* serpentine locomotion and similar to lateral undulation except used for crawling over soft crumbly sand where the entire body moves forward continuously

③ *concertina movement:* gripping or anchoring with portions of the body while pulling or pushing other sections in the direction of movement

④ *side-pushing:* irregular bends of the body and tail press vertically on the surface at different points; used to move across loose or slippery substrates

⑤ *rectilinear locomotion:* movement in a straight line where the belly scales are alternately lifted slightly from the ground and pulled forward, and then pulled downward and backward

Snakes can slither and slide in fast bursts on level and firm ground. They can reach up to 8 miles per hour (12.9 kph). Some snakes can move in quick bursts at speeds of 12 miles per hour (19.3 kph).[17]

• **Defense Mechanisms**

Snakes have numerous ways they defend themselves. Biting is generally a last-choice effort. **Coloration** often provides

excellent camouflage as they blend in exceptionally well in their natural environment. Also, some coloration patterns **mimic**

---

[17] The average person jogs at about 8 miles an hour.

(copy) that of a venomous snake, thus warning others not to bother.

Some snakes can, upon confrontation, burrow down under the sand or leaves for extra disguise or concealment. Some, like racers and coachwhips, will crawl away if they feel threatened. Most will stay quiet, coiled, or hidden as long as it is safe, hoping they are not seen. Some species will also mimic the rattlesnakes' practice of **tail-rattling**. This behavior includes those of rat snakes, bullsnakes, pine snakes, milk snakes, and kingsnakes. There is also the hognose snake, which, sometimes when under stress, will roll on its back and *play dead*. It can, however, come back viciously aggressive, so they are best left alone.

All snakes have **musk glands,** and most will use these as a means of self-defense. It allows the snake to ward off predators and other threats without having to fight. It also acts to discourage a predator and prevent being eaten by other animals. Younger and smaller snakes are more likely to use musk in the wild, but any snake can and will use it if feeling threatened. Musk is secreted from the cloacal scent gland (near the anus), which explains why it is often accompanied by urine and feces. It is a complicated mix of organic compounds. The stinky musk can smell almost as bad as that of a skunk's spray. Some have described snake musk's scent to be like that of foul rotten eggs or dead fish. Each snake species has its own unique musk smell.

Finally, many snakes' defense mechanisms include making themselves appear larger, puffing up, changing the appearance of the shape of their head, and threatening to

strike. Most snakes, however, are unlikely to attack or bite unless they are provoked. Most snake bites occur on people because someone failed to see the snake and either stepped on it or brushed up against it. Snakes are incredibly cautious of humans and are not prone to strike. A bite is their last-ditch effort to avoid harm. Merely leaving a snake alone in the landscape is the best way to avoid a bad encounter.

Reproduction

Snakes are solitary and do not form social bonds. Reproduction, however, causes a male snake to seek out a female. Those snakes in colder regions typically mate soon after emerging from brumation in early spring. This timing ensures that the young are born during warmer summer months. Snakes in warmer climates can mate year-round.

Mating is more of a race. The first snake to successfully wrap its tail around the female gets to mate. Male snakes, like some lizards, have a *pair* of sex organs, two penises called *hemipenes*.[18] Seventy percent (70%) of snakes are **oviparous,** meaning the offspring do not undergo any embryonic

---

[18] An *intromittent organ* is a general term for an external organ of a male specialized to deliver sperm during copulation.

development inside the mother. Eggs are laid, and in due time they hatch. The other 30 percent of snakes are **viviparous**, for their offspring develop into a

young animal *inside* the mother. This form of birth means that the mother snake simply keeps the eggs inside her until they are ready to hatch.

A snake could lay a clutch of eggs without mating in rare situations, but infertile eggs, called slugs, do not hatch. Such could even occur where a few *bad eggs* are laid amongst viable fertilized ones. Some species stay with their eggs until they hatch; however, most snakes do not. Those oviparous snakes generally just lay their eggs and then move on, and the baby snakes hatched never meet their mother. Upon birth, they immediately fend for themselves.

Snakes reach sexual maturity within two to four years, depending on the species and living conditions. In perfect conditions, adult snakes live anywhere from 20 to 30 years of age. Natural predators and human encroachment severely limit the number of years most snakes live. The oldest snake on record lived to be more than 42 years of age. Typically, it appears that the larger a snake can grow, the longer it can live.

Miscellaneous

As snakes grow, they have to shed their skin (called slough; pronounced *sloff* or *sluff*) because it no longer fits anymore or because it's old or worn out. When snakes grow, their skin does not, so they outgrow it. When this happens, they shed their outer layer of skin. These can be found in rock beds, log piles, and even tree branches (snakes can climb trees).

The shedding of skin, called **ecdysis** (or **molting**), is lost as one continuous piece. This event is under *hormonal control* and occurs four to 12 times per year. A healthy growing snake will generally molt once a month. The new skin is stretchable and allows for a larger body size than the previous covering. Younger snakes shed more often as they are in a more rapid growth phase. While shedding their skin is part of a

snake's growing process, it has another purpose as well. It aids in removing harmful parasites and bacteria. A snake will usually use some rough-textured surface in a higher humidity place to assist in wiggling out of their own skin.

The complete shedding process can take between one to two weeks. This period is a vulnerable time for a snake, and snakes are easily stressed during the shedding stage.

Snakes play essential roles in our natural ecosystems and should be respected and appreciated rather than feared. Snakes are important predators that help control rodent

ABOVE: Snake cuts off the air supply disabling the lizard. RIGHT: Snake prepares to swallow debilitated lizard..

populations that can spread diseases to humans. They are also important food sources for some birds, mammals, alligators[19], and even other snakes. Some non-venomous snakes, such as the Eastern Indigo Snake and Common Kingsnake[20], even eat venomous snakes!

Though humans fear snakes, snakes do not fear us; they just want to be left alone. We are much larger than they are, so they do not view us as prey but as a potential predator. **They will defend themselves if they feel threatened.** The best practice with snakes is to *admire them from a distance, be safe,* and *give it space.* If the snake gets agitated, walk away.

---

19 See *Love of Nature*, Issue 3: American Alligators & Crocodiles (2020). https://www.amazon.com/gp/product/B08CG6HB17/
20 Kingsnakes are immune to rattlesnake venom.

Snakes are here to serve a purpose in the ecosystem. One lesson to learn is that killing or removing nonvenomous snakes invites the venomous ones to move into the environment to take their place.

Endemic Nonvenomous Snakes in North America

(alphabetical)

Fifteen Most Common (in blue)

NAME		RANGE
Plains Black-head Snake		(predominately Colorado, Texas, Kansas, Nebraska, and Oklahoma)
California Mountain Kingsnake		(from CA north along the western slope of the Sierra Nevada Mountains into SW Oregon, southward in the eastern portion of Coast Ranges to the San Francisco Bay area, and south to north-central Baja California).
Coachwhip		(in SE North Carolina, SW Tennessee, extreme SE Illinois, extreme SW Nebraska, E Colorado, north-central New Mexico, SW Utah, west-central and S Nevada, central California, and S through Florida and Texas)

Common Garter Snake		(most widely distributed snake in North America).
Common King Snake		(from south New Jersey to South Florida and west to California and Mexico).
Corn Snake		(from south New Jersey south through Florida and west to Texas) and eastern Utah and western Colorado).
DeKay's Brown Snake		(from S Maine, S Quebec, and S Minnesota, south to Florida panhandle, and through Texas and Mexico to N Honduras).

Eastern Hognose Snake		(from eastern-central Minnesota to extreme S New Hampshire, south to S Florida, west to E Texas and W Kansas), slightly upturned snout).
Eastern Indigo Snake		(all areas of the southeastern U.S.)
Snake Eastern Ribbon Snake		(all areas of the eastern U.S., except northern New England).
Glossy Snake		(from SE Texas and extreme SW Nebraska west to central California, south into Mexico).

Gopher Snake		(with subspecies, found in most parts of the US).
Long-nosed Snake		(from SW Kansas, SE Colorado, and New Mexico south into Mexico and NW to Arizona, W Utah, Nevada, and central California).
Milk Snake		(from SE Maine, S Wisconsin, central and southeast Minnesota south through most of the U.S. east of the Rocky Mountains).
Mud Snake		(from SE Virginia to S Florida, west to E Texas, and north in Mississippi Valley to S Illinois).

Night Snake		(from north-central California, south-central Washington, S Idaho, Utah, and SW Kansas south through Baja California).
Northern Water Snake		(from Maine to the coast of North Carolina and south to Georgia and Alabama).
Pine Snake		(with subspecies, found in most of the western US and also in the southeast.
Plain-bellied Water Snake		(from S Delaware to N Florida, west through Alabama to W Texas and southeast New Mexico, north to W Missouri and S Illinois and Indiana).

Plains Black-headed Snake		(from S Nebraska south through W Kansas and E Colorado to S Texas, New Mexico, SE Arizona, and into Mexico).
Prairie Kingsnake		(from central Maryland to north Florida, west to SE Nebraska and E Texas).
Queen Snake		(found in most parts of the eastern US except New England and Florida).
Racer		(in every state in the continental U.S., except Alaska).

Rainbow Snake		(from S Maryland south to central Florida, and west to Mississippi River).
Rat Snake		(from E Ontario and S Vermont south to the Florida Keys, west to W Texas, north to SW Minnesota and S Michigan).
Red-bellied Snake		(from SE Saskatchewan to Nova Scotia, south to central Florida, and west to E Texas).
Ringneck Snake		(from Nova Scotia to the Florida Keys, west to the Pacific coast, south to central Mexico).

Rosy Boa[21]		(from S California into N Baja California and SW Arizona).
Rubber Boa		(from British Columbia to S California, eastward to Montana, Wyoming, and Utah.
Striped Whipsnake		(from south-central Washington to S New Mexico and west and central Texas).
Western Hognose Snake		(from SE Alberta and NW Manitoba south to SE Arizona, Texas, and into N Mexico).

---

[21] Only two boa constrictors are native to North America: Rubber Boa and Rosy Boa.

Western Shovel-nosed Snake		(from south-central Nevada south into Baja California).

REVIEW

1. Why do you believe most people are afraid of snakes?

2. What is the difference between poisonous and venomous?

3. Why do you think most people believe snakes are slimy?

4. List three characteristics of non-venomous snakes?

5. What tool do biologists use to identify organisms?

6. Why is identifying snakes challenging to do?

7. List three characteristics often used to identify venomous from non-venomous snakes?

8. What kinds of food do snakes eat?

9. How does a snake swallow something larger than itself?

10. What is brumation and how does it affect a snake?

RAT SNAKE EATING A MOUSE

COLORING PAGE

http://www.supercoloring.com/coloring-pages/corn-snake-devouring-dead-mouse?version=print

Name: _______________________

Non-venomous Snakes: Slithering Reptiles

Carefully read each sentence or statement. Write the correct answer in each appropriate box.
Use the word bank if necessary.

brumation   ligaments   scutes   maxilla   threatened   viviparous   ecdysis   constrictor

poikilotherm   dicotomous   venomous   herpetology

Across

2. Sleep but not sleep; just lethargic.
4. Quadrate bone opens widely by way of

____

5. Appears to be live birth but simply holds the eggs internally?
7. Type of snake that squeezes the life out of its prey?
8. Study of reptiles and amphibians
10. Most snakes do NOT attack unless feel

__________.

11. Description of the 'key' used to identify animals and other organisms?
12. Shedding of skin; form of molting?

Down

1. Another name for 'jawbone.'
3. cold-blooded
6. scales
9. The presence of non-venomous snakes also can mean the fewer _________ snakes around.

INTERESTING SOURCES TO CONSIDER

11 non-venomous snakes you want in your backyard. Available at:
https://www.chron.com/neighborhood/slideshow/11-non-venomous-snakes-you-want-in-your-backyard-193573.php

Cottonmouth 7/2020. Available at:
https://youtu.be/g6V5X0BEmaE

Cottonmouth vs Water Snake! Brave Wilderness. Available at:
https://youtu.be/1oa6VziZH78

Cottonmouth vs. Water Snakes: How To Spot The Difference! (ft. Life's Wild Adventures). Available at:
https://youtu.be/QuBlajsf714

Fact or Fiction? Test Your Knowledge About Snakes. Available at: https://www.livescience.com/50583-snake-facts.html

Facts you should know about nonvenomous snakes. Available at:
https://bit.ly/2H9cIfs

Florida's Nonvenomous Snakes. Available at:
https://cityofwinterpark.org/docs/departments/parks-recreation/lakes/health-safety-regarding-recreational-use-lakes-central-florida/nonvenomous-snake-guide.pdf

Harmless snakes avoid danger by mimicking the triangular heads of vipers. National Genographic. Available at:
https://on.natgeo.com/3f6kByI

How to tell the difference between venomous vs. non-venomous snakes. Available at: https://bit.ly/3kDZZPy

Snake Facts: Non-Venomous Snakes. Available at: https://snake-facts.weebly.com/non-venomous.html

Snakes of Texas (Pt. 1): Awesome Desert Snakes! Available at:
https://youtu.be/d1UgikDC6Oc

What to Do When You See a Snake. Available at:
https://youtu.be/dlY5wimKr9s

ABOUT THE AUTHOR

Richard NeSmith is a native of Florida, USA. He grew up wading through the swamps of central Florida with his two younger brothers during the pre-Disney era, and unknowingly falling in love with biology, wildlife, and nature. He has lived in seven American states, twice in Australia and once in Mexico City. He holds eight university degrees and has taught for 14 years in secondary schools, here and abroad, and another 13 years as a professor in several American universities. His service includes professor of science education, Dean of Education, Campus Dean, and an online instructor. His passion for learning (and *how we learn*) did not develop until *after* graduating from high school. His only explanation for this is that *having a goal made all the difference in the world.* He enjoys reading, hiking, nature photography, golf, tennis, and RV camping.

http://richardnesmith.obior.cc

Applied Principles of Education & Learning *presents*

APE-Learning

AMAZON AUTHOR's PAGE:

https://www.amazon.com/author/richardnesmith

Educational, wildlife, and naturalist books
Dr. Richard NeSmith.

Issue 1
Raccoons:
Friendly Bandits
Dr. Richard NeSmith

Issue 2
Sandhill Cranes
&
Pileated Woodpeckers
Flaming Redheads
Dr. Richard NeSmith

Issue 3
American
Alligators
&
Crocodiles
Dr. Richard NeSmith

Issue 4
Bobcats:
Ghostly Elusive
Dr. Richard NeSmith

Issue 5
Foxes:
Sneaky Rascals
Dr. Richard NeSmith

Issue 6
Armadillo:
Little Armored One
Dr. Richard NeSmith

Issue 7
Squirrels:
Bushy-Tail Scampers
Dr. Richard NeSmith

Issue 8
River Otters:
Aquatic Clowns!
Dr. Richard NeSmith

Issue 9
Beavers:
Nature's Engineers !
Dr. Richard NeSmith

Issue 10
Black Bears
Titans of the Forest
Dr. Richard NeSmith

Issue 11
Freshwater
Turtles
Dr. Richard NeSmith

Issue 12
FUNGI, LICHENS
& MUSHROOMS
Dr. Richard NeSmith

Paperbacks: http://amazon.com/author/richardnesmith

e-books: https://bit.ly/3iuCgB3

---

[i] **Special thanks to the following who kindly provided permission to use their photographs.**

From Unsplash: Waldemar Brandt,

From Pixabay: Karsten Paulick, Sipa, Nature-Pix, WikiImages, Josch13, Anrita, Paul Brennan, Filip Kruchlik, PublicDomainPictures,

Also, special thanks to **Stacey Diamond**, **Denise Sult**, **Randy Johnson**, **Tom Dotson**, **Cindy Frasier**, **DS Damm**, **Destiny Allen**, for their graciously sharing of some photographs of these beautiful creatures.

Thank you, everyone.

Love Learning –Love Nature—Love Living